Snippets of a Spotless Mind

Bryan Patrick Holland

BookLeaf Publishing

India | USA | UK

Presentation by *BookLeaf Publishing*

Web: www.bookleafpub.com

E-mail: info@bookleafpub.com

ISBN: 9789358367560

First edition 2023

Mom and Dad, for always supporting my crazy endeavors (or being the voice of reason when they are too crazy)

ACKNOWLEDGEMENT

I'd like to thank my entire family, my friends, Incubus, well-made tacos, Tom Robbins, the absurd universe and planet we call home, and of course, BookLeaf Publishing for putting this idea into my head. Thank you.

PREFACE

The idea behind this book was to write one poem a day for 21 days. Sometimes I had a lot to say, others were short, others geared towards music. I've decided in the past year that I want to take my creativity and challenge it, push it further, get more experimental with all of it. This is a product of that idea. I hope you enjoy.

General Omniscient Deity

What is God?
Something's there
But what is it?
When and where?
The Earth, the stars,
The moon and sun,
Were all created
by just one?
Could it be
Just energy?
And possibly in
You and me?
Whatever it is
It can be seen
In practically
Everything
But why would God create hate?
And why would God allow rape?
Why would God let them kill
And base our lives on dollar bills?
Maybe it's us
Who made all the bad
Maybe it's us
Who make ourselves sad
Maybe if we

Would try to give up
All the negativity
And blowing things up
Maybe if we
would let peace be
with no controversy
over whose God is supreme

Thrive Inn

Let this be
a level-headed letter to myself,
Exactly what I need
when I take it off the shelf,
This wealth
you've been chasing in Hell,
Your health
Is at the bottom of the well.
Set sail
and say "Sell! Sell! Sell!"
Simplify and minimize
Or hear the death bell,
Cracked shell
Filling a void,
Never enough
When your love's unemployed.

The eye of the storm is crying
I'm vibing all night at the Thrive Inn.

Wings in the Wind

It was 2 am and -15 degrees
When I noticed the first one.
Subtle at first
A smoky and sleeping wisp
Whipping across the frosted pavement
Real fast
Shadows in the whiteout dancing in and out of
the sparkling mandala-like snowflakes
Snow upon the road being tossed upward and
floating all about, providing cover for the
prowling, alien silhouettes.
I drove along the snaking roadway
Aware of my neck hair standing at attention
Like a frequency in the air buzzed along my
spine and awoke the innate electric within me.
I'm the only one out here.
It feels like the end of the world has already
happened and I'm driving alone within the
remnants of a civilization
Being flung about, angry and confused
I'm still here

Can't Force A Heart To Love

Some say they see
A heart
Unfinished piece of art,
Faded edges of
long forgotten pledges
Some say…
Some stay…
Some go away

Spade

You'll find that your heart blooms like a lotus
when you dig deeper
Into the webs of neurons the brain reads
Like a new novel from its favorite author
Excitedly page turning your way
into an everlasting tale
Weaving the bounties you've reaped
through what you've sown

Wizard Tree

Seeing is believing.
But our eyes and brain are in cahoots
to find the quickest route
Just fill in the gaps logically
But that logic is
based off limited experiences
varying from person to person
So I say and see
a lot I don't understand
I don't need to understand it
from any vantage point
other than
"it's true to those who believe it."

Electric Flow

The electricity flows through the mountains and
it knows,
That the current state of the world shows
There's a lot more to this life than we know,
so like water, it helps, it grows
like the improvised words of this prose

Doors

Cloudy connections and confession
are bound to astral inject them
selves toward perfection
but in each dimension
it's been said in sacred texts when
you let go of that desire to be what you are not
you're now seeing the doors of perception
leading you there
where you belonged
all along

Either Way

She pushed herself away
 Then she called out my name
it's a silly game we play
it's all the same
either way
it's always the same

She hightails into town
to feel the lights and sound
to find herself again
she's looking for a friend
lookin for…
either way
it's always the same

On the road back home
she reaching for that phone
drunk and thinking of our song
it takes so long to be gone
either way
it's always the same

A Snooze Button For Rooster

When you're known for something
It can be tiresome
Fulfilling
That identity
People
Amongst other things
Evolve, change and grow
New skin

Learning and yearning
to sleep in
the field of dreams
Clocks tick tock
Time won't stop
Burning
New me
Alarm sound off
Dreaming
Good morning

Let it go

Sitting by a river
watching the ripples flow
while the wind gently blows
I'm looking into your eyes
I've looked into a thousand times

I don't know how to say this
but we need to just choose a road
and let it go
or let it flow

Questions arise in your eyes
But the answers they are not words
We've been crossing this street so many times
I can't even choose a side no more

So let it go
I don't know
let me know
let it go
let it flow

Once in Awhile

Every now and then
I'm looking for a friend
one that I can lean on
when I'm stuck around the bend
a friend is all you need
when family can't suffice
when your demons are the heavy breed
holding you under frozen ice
so be that unto others
since you may one day need
a new sister or a brother
to help you stop the bleed

Braced by Beauty

When someone has your back
You have more spine
Sounds change perspectives and moods
When things aren't going well
Reach out
To the friends and music
That doesn't bail when it's bad

hard. left.

90 degrees and my world changed
180 nothing stays the same
270 nearing the end game
360 full circle we came

please

quick from the jump off
it's a short tune
fill it up with cleverness
and pump it full of ruin
sadness causes static
causing me to meditate
logic dissipated.
there's no need to hesitate
since there was a mission
I was sent here to believe in
I've been clawing and retrieving
and receiving all the demons
sick, a spotless mind
eternal sunshine for every dark side of life

I clear my head with a symphony of sounds
that are coming from the ground to the skies and
all around.
please

Rose Galaxy

It's fun to scream out loud.
But no-one does it. Not at home.
Less in public.
Sometimes you've got to release that energy.
It's the nebula inside, wanting to manifest.
To be born,
screaming through the chasms and flame into
bright existence.
Seeking love by giving love.

When we dream

When we dream
where does our mind go?
Our soul?
Is it thinking of me? (Or me thinking?)
Or are we already there?

Startled Headdress

a shaman is inside of you
the playful mystic with a wandering eye,
and an innate ability to let their nature be that of
nature.
Wide-eyed.
seemingly mesmerized
Potion. I died
Generally fight or flight says yes,
that is true.
Maybe alert and aware works too
Spooked
being in his body on this plane,
soaring through darkness with one lightbulb, and
when it goes out what is next?

anyone truly aware and alert
in this existence
balances awe
and
being scared shitless

Never enough

You ever catch that feeling
where anxiety is creeping
and you can't shake off the demons
Aura's static and it's screaming?
No matter what you do
there's a message there for you
When you're hiding from the truth
you freeze deciding what to do
So I dig and I claw til my paws bleed red
this existential dread
Yes it echoes in my head
It's feeding on me believing
the deceiving ego thing
needing people needing me

Discovering the loving things will always bring me back
When I'm hovering above these things I always fall right
back
it's where I lack
The cards are stacked
I'm stumbling and crumbling when things get out of
whack
So I sedate, and isolate,
take the weight up off my shoulders
Tempting fate as I grow older

And I wait
procrastinate
hurt the ones around me
Never there or very late

See, this indecision is a prison
And the numbness doesn't listen
Hazy visions of a mission
But I'm watching television
Secret I've been missing, something
Shooting star wishing, veil of Maya lifting

Sifting through the ash of burning cash
Never enough
When you're grinding every day and there's still mad bills
to pay
Just waiting in vain for each pay day
Never enough
When you're scrolling on your phone and you're sitting
home alone
and you should be getting things done
Never enough
When it's 6 in the morning and you find yourself calling
the guy who's holding
Never enough
And you've been thinking that your drinking isn't helping
you believe in anything
You lost that feeling
Never enough
Each and every single thing

Sifting through the ash of burning cash

Precious moments pass on by while your life doesn't feel
right
So you try and try and try and try to
Find your purpose
you try to find your tribe
There's a bridge here, dopamine seeking, devour fiending
Consuming and consuming til the void is receding
Consuming and consuming and we let it keep bleeding
And we're fuming at the idea that it's us disappearing

Since I can remember
I've been trying to fill a void
Devour fiending
Dopamine seeking
Each and every single thing
And we're fuming that it's us disappearing
Never enough
Goodbye please

Elm St.

There is no such thing as good vibes only.
There's no such thing as good vibes only.
Talk to success
evil does dwell on it
and as soon as you face it,
the better off you'll be.
Fear is the cause of many of man's evolutions.
Revolution and survival, mainly out of the fear
of death.
But acceptance and inclusion
of the duality inherent in nature
is key to getting the ability
to ride the waves when they surge
as well as when they crash.
Look at your fear, and let it touch you.
Grow from it.
Go and evolve in the nearest way
be better, leave things better off
for the future evolvers

What beckons you from your dreams? What are
you afraid of that your nightmares reveal? Face
them. With all you can and then show someone
else how to face theirs. With love.

her

Her hair flows like a wavy blonde ocean,
a picture of her face sets my heart back in
motion